W9-BXX-565

The Lightning Dreamer

The Lightning Dreamer

Cuba's Greatest Abolitionist

MARGARITA ENGLE

Houghton Mifflin Harcourt

Boston   New York

www.hmhco.com

Text set in Perpetua.

The Library of Congress has cataloged the hardcover edition as follows:
Engle, Margarita.
The lightning dreamer : Cuba's greatest abolitionist / Margarita Engle.
p. cm.
Summary: In free verse, evokes the voice of Gertrudis Gomez de Avellaneda, a
book-loving writer, feminist, and abolitionist who courageously fought injustice in
nineteenth-century Cuba. Includes historical notes, excerpts from her writings,
biographical information, and source notes.
Includes bibliographical references: page .
1. Gómez de Avellaneda y Arteaga, Gertrudis, 1814–1873—Juvenile fiction.
[1. Novels in verse. 2. Gómez de Avellaneda y Arteaga, Gertrudis, 1814–1873—
Fiction. 3. Authors—Fiction. 4. Feminists—Fiction. 5. Abolitionists—Fiction.
6. Cuba—History—1810–1899—Fiction.] I. Title.
PZ7.5.E54Lig 2013
[Fic]—dc23
2013003913

ISBN: 978-0-547-80743-0 hardcover
ISBN: 978-0-544-54112-2 paperback

Manufactured in the United States of America
DOC 10 9 8 7 6 5 4 3 2 1
4500547372

For young writers in search of words

El esclavo ha dejado volar libre su pensamiento, y su pensamiento subía más allá de las nubes en que se forma el rayo.

The slave let his mind fly free, and his thoughts soared higher than the clouds where lightning forms.

— *Gertrudis Gómez de Avellaneda*

Contents

Historical Background

In the United States, Northern abolitionists were able to speak out against slavery in public. The Spanish colony of Cuba was different. With no part of the island free of slavery, censorship was harsh and penalties severe. The most daring abolitionists were poets who could veil their work with metaphors. Of these, the boldest was a young woman named Gertrudis Gómez de Avellaneda. Her childhood nickname was Tula.

Part One
Suns and Rays

1827

Tula

Books are door-shaped
portals
carrying me
across oceans
and centuries,
helping me feel
less alone.

But my mother believes
that girls who read too much
are unladylike
and ugly,
so my father's books are locked
in a clear glass cabinet. I gaze
at enticing covers
and mysterious titles,
but I am rarely permitted
to touch
the enchantment
of words.

Poems.

Stories.

Plays.

All are forbidden.

Girls are not supposed to think,

but as soon as my eager mind

begins to race, free thoughts

rush in

to replace

the trapped ones.

I imagine distant times

and faraway places.

Ghosts.

Vampires.

Ancient warriors.

Fantasy moves into

the tangled maze

of lonely confusion.

Secretly, I open

an invisible book in my mind,

and I step

through its magical door-shape

into a universe

of dangerous villains

and breathtaking heroes.

Many of the heroes are men

and boys, but some are girls

so tall

strong

and clever

that they rescue other children

from monsters.

Manuel

My big sister tells
bizarre fantasy tales,
acting them out in whispers
beneath a jungle of leaves
in the shady garden.

Her stories of powerful giants
and terrifying beasts
turn the evening
into a forest
of secrets.

I leave the garden feeling
as if I have traveled
to a distant land.

If only our real lives
could be as heroic as her tales
of courageous giants
one hundred heads high.

Tula

I've trained my little brother

to be a brave smuggler of words.

He hides his schoolbooks

under my embroidery hoop

one

forbidden

volume

at a time

so that our frowning mother

and scolding stepfather

hardly ever grow

suspicious.

When no one is looking,

I seize one of Manuel's books

and flee to the garden,

where words

glitter

and glow

in starlight.

Tula

I am thirteen now, so close
to the age of forced marriage
that invented worlds
made of words
are my only
comfort.

I try to explain my fear
of a loveless wedding
to Mamá, but her mind
is busy with greedy
visions . . .

If only she could dream
of her own future
instead of mine.

Mamá

Thirteen! It is the age for dreams
of sparkling jewels and silken gowns
in elegant ballrooms . . .
not hideous fantasies
about ferocious beasts.

Everyone knows that girls
who read and write too much
are unattractive. Men want
quiet females who listen,
not loud ones who offer
opinions.

Tula

Thirteen is the age for dreams
of changing the world
by freeing my own heart.

Thirteen is a barefoot rider
on a naturally graceful horse,
with no fierce spurs, heavy saddle,
iron bit, or vicious reins
to control the mouth
and the mind.

People assume that men
make all the rules, but sometimes
mothers are the ones who command
girls to be quiet
while they arrange
for us to be sold
like oxen
or mules.

Tula

I feel like a new person
when I play make-believe games
in the garden, inventing tales
of monsters and heroes.

Mamá commands me to hush,
and my stepfather grumbles,
so I try to be quiet,
but silence feels
like an endless
echoing
hallway
of smooth
shiny mirrors
that reflect
my ragged
impatience.

I end up growling and roaring
like a beast.

Mamá

Why does my stubborn daughter
bellow and howl each time I tell her
to stop being so loud
and so rude?

I'm just doing my motherly
duty — why can't she listen to a voice
of sensible reason?

Doesn't she see that her future
is my future, and little Manuel's?
Without Tula's help in achieving
a successful marriage for herself,
no one in this family will ever
possess the sheer power
of great wealth.

Tula

On lonely nights, I remember
my father, who allowed me to read
as much as I wanted.
While he was alive, I felt
like my brother's equal. I felt human.

I never had to challenge absurd rules
by smashing a glass bookcase,
just to steal a glance
at hidden pages.

Now, when Mamá catches me
with a book in my hands and shards
of glass on my shoes, she sends me
to my silent room, where I spend
quiet hours remembering
the freedom
to read.

Tula

Shortly before my birth, Papá saw
the head of a rebellious slave
paraded on a stake. The poor man's
hands were nailed to trees; his limbs
tumbled outside
churchyard gates . . .

The sight made Papá furious.
He was a soldier, but he'd learned
to detest violence,
growing ill with sorrow
each time he heard rumors
of warfare.

Without slavery, he concluded,
there would be no more fighting,
no anger or dread.
He dreamed of returning
to his birthplace in Spain,

and in preparation,

he freed our old cook,

paying her a fair wage

instead of keeping her in chains.

Caridad

I've been the only cook, maid,
seamstress, gardener, and nanny
in this family
for at least a thousand years.

Vaya—oh well, it certainly feels
like a thousand, even if it's only
thirty or forty. Some years feel
so much longer than others—slower,
deeper, more powerful.
The year when Tula first began
telling me her far-fetched stories
was one of those times.
She was only nine.

Now we sit together often,
dreaming of heroic giants
who can defeat bloodsucking
vampires.

Tula

When Caridad and I peer
through the bars of a window,
we see weary slave girls trudging
along the rough cobblestone street,
with enormous baskets
of pineapples and coconuts
balanced on their heads.

Sometimes I feel as if
I can trade my thoughts
for theirs. Are we really
so different, with our heavy
array of visible
and invisible
burdens?

Tula

When fever
took Papá,
I folded
my sorrow
into words,
one tiny
leaf
of paper,
my first
raging poem
of loss.

Now each glimpse
of a slave girl's suffering
turns into one more
hidden
verse.

Tula

Mamá does not permit me
to attend school like Manuel,
so a tutor comes to the house,
instructing me in music and art.
For lessons in embroidery
and saints' lives, I go to the convent,
where veiled nuns permit me
to read mysterious tales
of hermits, martyrs, and beasts,
like the story about Santa Margarita,
who was swallowed by a dragon.

Each day, after my lessons, the nuns
let me visit their marvelous library,
where I feel as if I have entered
heaven on earth.

Caridad

The poems Tula recites
fall onto my ears
like shooting stars
or flowers
in a storm wind,
plummeting toward earth
instead of drifting.

Each verse is an arrow
piercing my past — the years
of bondage that prevented me
from learning to read
while I was young.

Tula says it's never too late,
but I'm old, and I'm so very tired,
and I have too much work . . .

The Nuns

We read all manner of verse and prose
forbidden to other females.

For Tula to gain the freedom to enjoy
unlimited reading later in life,
she will have to take vows and join us.
Beyond these convent gates, books
are locked away
and men
hold
the keys.

For now, Tula seems content
to roam our peaceful library,
growing breathless
with the excitement
of a youthful mind's
natural curiosity.

Tula

In a dusty corner
of the convent library,
I discover the banned books
of José María Heredia, a rebel-poet—
an abolitionist and *independista*
who was forced into exile.

His verses show that he believes
in Cuba's freedom from Spain,
as well as liberty for slaves.
When I take the verses home
to Caridad, she weeps.

I cannot tell if her tears pour
from a fountain of hope
for the unknowable future
or sorrows left over
from an unchangeable past.

Caridad

Certain poems
help me feel young
instead of old.

Powerful
instead of weak.

Brave
instead of fearful.

Their words are like wings,
helping me fly away
from this kitchen,
this mop,
these filthy pots and pans,
my endless chores . . .

The Nuns

Heredia's verses are banned
by the Crown, not the Church,
so we feel free to read them.
We knew him well.

He was already a poet while he
was just a young boy. Some people
are born with words flowing
in their veins.

At fifteen, Heredia wrote a play.
At nineteen, he became a member
of *los Soles y Rayos* — the Suns and Rays
of Bolívar, a secret society of poets
and artists who hoped to establish
a democratic nation of equals,
with no masters or slaves,
and one vote per man,
dark or light.

Tula

I will never grow tired
of exploring Heredia's poetry.

Here is a verse
about being at sea
alone
in a storm.

And here is one about hiking
beside an immense waterfall
called Niágara.

And listen to this poem
about refusing to accept
the existence of slavery
and refusing to see all of nature
as good and beautiful,
with the sole
exception
of human nature.

Caridad

Heredia is pale
and has always been free,
just like Tula.

Somehow, with words
from wild poems
floating
all around me,
I feel certain that words
can be as human
as people,
alive
with the breath
of compassion.

Tula

Whispered words
about the Suns and Rays
continue to fascinate me.
The nuns tell me that Heredia's
secret society had even designed
a flag — deep blue, with a gold sun
at the center, and a human face
on the sun, to remind us that people
can glow.

Each ray of the round sun
is just a narrow sliver,
but together
all the tiny rays
join to release
a single
enormous
horizon of light.

Tula

Heredia's poems haunt me.
From my room, I watch the march
of chained slave children
as they pass beyond
the carved
wooden bars
of my window.

In the kitchen, I listen
to the knife-beat
spoon-beat
pounding
songs
of Caridad.

Then I eat my guilty dinner,
wondering how many slaves
Mamá will buy with the money
she gains by marrying me to
the highest bidder.

Tula

At night, the view
from my window changes.

Horses gallop
along the cobblestones.

There are gunshots
and screams.

Will there be another
rebellion
with heads
paraded on stakes
and hands
nailed to trees?

Tula

When no one is watching,
I carry a basket of fruit
on my head, just to find out
how it feels to need
balance.

I chop an onion.
Stir a soup.
Sweep a floor.
Frown.

Then I fill the air of the garden
with Heredia's floating rhymes,
and soon I'm reciting a few poems
of my own, while Caridad
listens
beneath the silent
moon and stars.

Tula

Visions! The night is filled
with fierce spirits and gentle ones.
Invisible beings spin and moan.
Floor, ceiling, and walls
whisper, wail, and shout . . .
Phantoms beg me to transform
my strange dreams
into stories.
Words burst
and fly
past trees
in the garden.
I rise up out of a nightmare
and grasp a feather pen,
feeling winged.

Manuel

Feather pens, flowing ink,
and weightless paper—
they mean
nothing at all to me.

So I give them away
to my sister, who claims
she feels trapped
and can free herself only
with words.

Tula

When we visit my grandfather

on his sugar plantation,

I see how luxurious

my mother's childhood

must have been,

surrounded by beautiful

emerald green sugar fields

harvested

by row after row

of sweating slaves.

How can one place

be so lovely

and so sorrowful

all at the same time?

Tula

My grandfather speaks
of the various noblemen
he might select for me
next year, when I reach
the dreaded age
of fourteen.

Twice, my mother defied her father
in order to marry for love, but now
she expects me to regain her place
in my grandfather's will
by marrying a stranger
in exchange
for gold.

Tula

On our last day in the countryside,
my grandfather gives me a cruel gift:

a yellow songbird
flapping helplessly
inside a delicate
bamboo cage.

The captive bird's
graceful wings
are useless.

All it can do is flutter
and sing.

Part Two

The Orphan
Theater

1827

Tula

My pen is empty.
I cannot write.

All I do is watch
my caged goldfinch
and listen to his brave
little song.

I have discovered injustice,
but what good is a witness
who cannot testify?

I am silent.
Useless.
My voice
has vanished.

Will I ever learn how to sing
on paper?

Tula

My indoor world of walls
grows so quiet that I have to create
my own noise.

I recite Heredia's poems of justice
out loud.

Mamá calls me a land of extremes.
My stepfather covers his ears.
Do they imagine that I enjoy
swaying back and forth
between moods of flame
and ice?

If only I could be calm, like my bird,
who waits all night for morning sun.

If only I could be
someone else.

Tula

Opinions.
Ideas.
Possibilities.
So many!
How can I choose?
Between bursts
of lightning-swift energy,
I enjoy peaceful moments
when the whole world
seems to be a flowing river
of verse
and all I have to do is learn
how to swim.

During those times,
I find it so easy to forget
that I'm just a girl who is expected
to live
without thoughts.

Tula

I speak my mind, and then
I have to apologize to Mamá
over and over, always the same
sincere apology. I really am sorry,
so sorry that I am not
the sort of daughter
my mother can love.

When she catches me writing,
she calls me sinful, *loca* — crazy —
a manly girl, a madwoman,
monstrous . . .

She warns me that no rich man
will ever fall in love with a girl
who loves books, but I don't care.
I will never marry a man
who thinks girls
should be
stupid.

The Nuns

Tula comes to us
with her dilemma.

Her choices
are narrow.

In a mother's eyes,
she can be only
a monster of defiance
or an angel of obedience,
nothing
in between.

So we send her to the library,
a safe place to heal
and dream . . .

Tula

Each time I read the freedom verses
of Heredia, I become more and more
aware of poor old Caridad's
horrifying youth.

She was a slave.
She belonged to my family.
There is nothing I can do
to give back those lost years,
but I do have a voice.
I can speak of her
sorrows
on paper.

Tula

I study verses with a drumbeat rhythm
like pounding music.

Other poems are sea waves, calm
and soothing.

Just as often, poetry is a free
dance
    of birds in air
        swooping
            and dipping
in surprising
    directions.

I discover a mystery
in each verse;
the stillness
between words.

Tula

Counted lines of sorrow for a sonnet.
Rapidly rhymed beats of fury.

My own verses soon flow,
shrieking and groaning
from my smuggled pen.

I walk with empty hands,
letting the rhythm of footsteps
turn into silence or bird song—
I never know which to expect.

Time and distance vanish.
    I feel lopsided
        like a tree that reaches
           toward sunlight
        rising from a rooted forest
    of buried truths.
I feel the mysterious power
of growth.

Tula

When I ask Caridad
about her childhood,
she will not answer.

It is as if she owns
a hidden gift
that she refuses
to share.

I can't really blame her.
I imagine that in her place,
I would keep my own outraged
treasury of secrets.

Just think how many
papery secrets
I already own.

Tula

Am I crazy, foolish, confused?
Do any of my poems make sense?

I burn my verses in the same oven
where Caridad bakes spicy cakes
before decorating them with sweet
coconut frosting.

My brother gives me more of his
enchanted paper, but I tell him
the magic has vanished.

The kitchen air grows thick
with soot and smoke, the remains
of my words inhaled as we breathe
the ashes of my poems.

I don't know how to destroy
the invisible part
of a verse.

The Nuns

We seek a way to cheer Tula.
Caring for others would help her
forget her own troubles,
so we remind her
that treating other people
the way she hopes to be treated
is God's golden rule.

Soon she is dreaming
of a thousand ways to help
beggars, lepers, the blind . . .

But her most original idea
is the one she finally chooses,
an entertaining and educational
theater
for orphans.

Tula

Silenced.

Censored.

Ignored.

Home is a place

of mute limitations,

but at the convent orphanage,

far from my mother,

I can shout

and sing!

Here, no one calls me "professor"

when I quote a wise poem, or "atheist"

if I question

traditional ways.

In the company of orphans,

I feel free of my family's

impossible

expectations.

Tula

Manuel is my chaperone,
walking me back and forth
to the orphanage. Without a brother
to escort me, I would truly feel
imprisoned.
I'm glad that I'm not
a real orphan, and I do love my mother,
I do, but I wish she could understand
my despair.

Why can't she see that no two people
are exactly alike? Our hearts and minds
are all different.
Only our dreams share
this same desperate need
to rise
and soar . . .

Tula

At the orphan theater, my plays
about evil vampires and heroic giants
are not considered suitable
by the nuns, who must endure
their own mute limitations.

So I learn to write quiet scenes
about ordinary places and real people.

Even without fantasy, my words
grow and change
into something
truly inventive
because here, all the actors
are lonely children
who know how to create
their own magic.

Tula

At home, I sing and hum,
preparing for the next day's
rehearsal.

In the kitchen, Caridad's cakes
bring memories of the way
I used to cook with her
when I was little.

Mamá expected a solemn kitchen,
but Caridad let me sing
while I stirred.

When the cakes were done,
we both ate our fill, but the cook
and I
had to sit at separate tables
in different rooms.

Caridad

When I was young,
I ran away
over and over
but slave hunters
always caught me
and brought me back
to this house.

Now, when Tula asks why
I stayed here after her father
finally freed me,
I have no answer,
just the memory
of fear.

Tula

Poetry is all I have to give.
I don't know any other way
to help.

Even though Caridad
is busy in the kitchen,
I feel certain
that she listens
as she swirls
her copper spoon
through a bubbling stew.

Words find their own way
into the shared rhythms
of our separate lives.

Tula

I continue to dream up my own
set of rules — for life, for poetry,
for the orphan theater.

In my plays, all are equal.
Each orphan receives
a speaking role,
because every child
has a voice that must be heard,
even if adults only listen
while children are perched
on a stiff wooden stage,
chirping like new-hatched birds
that have not yet learned
how to sing.

The Orphans

Tula's theater is merciful.
It helps us forget who we are.

We stitch costumes of scraps,
decorated with beads
of laughter.

We paint wooden sunsets
and the false fronts
of imaginary houses.

Each swoop of a paintbrush
turns into our own magical
dance
of celebration.

Tula

The orphans speak
in unique ways,
no two alike.

Some use silence,
the visible language
of brooding eyes.

Others dream up new words
born of boredom or humor.

The shy ones offer nothing
but shrugs and gestures,
a ballet
of graceful hands.

My own voice bursts like an ember,
releasing wild sparks
of surprise.

Manuel

At home in the shadowy garden,
my sister performs a secret play —
a dangerous one — *El campesino
espantado* (*The Frightened
Country Boy*), written by Heredia
when he was only fifteen.

It's a funny play, yet serious too,
the tale of a farm boy who visits
a crowded city. When a coachman
wants payment for a carriage ride,
the country boy is shocked,
because he is accustomed to
wagon rides that are freely given
by lonely farmers, who are eager
to chat on and on about cows,
chickens, weather, and the phases
of the mysterious moon.

In the city, the country boy

tries to help a runaway slave,
but his efforts fail, and both he
and the slave are hunted
and punished.

Later, the country boy is robbed
and falsely accused of murder.

In the end, he returns to his farm,
where all the snorting, clucking,
bleating animals
make so much more sense
than people.

The play is clearly a tale
of injustice. I fear for my sister
and for our whole family. If Tula
is caught reciting the rebel-poems
of Heredia, will we all
be arrested
and tortured?

Caridad

After the final meal of the day,
I sit on a bench in the garden,
where my thoughts
are my own
until Tula's young voice
invades them.

While I listen to her play-acted
tales of injustice, I begin to feel
that maybe I should run free
just one more time
before this entire household
is punished.

Tula

I'm tired of being told
that my feelings are too wild.
I argue with Manuel when he says
I'm too bold. Why shouldn't
hilarious scenes make me dizzy
with laughter, unfair ones hurl me
into a rage, and sad ones fill me
with grief for the imagined
suffering
of fictional characters?

I can't help plunging
into the heart of each line
just as thoroughly
as if all the dreams
and disappointments
were my own.

The Orphans

We feel transformed.
Each word of each play
helps us imagine
distant lives.

Scenes that make the nuns cry
leave us smiling behind our
veiled curtain
of wishes.

We long to try new tales,
even the forbidden ones
about giants and vampires
with unnatural skills.

We are always eager to play
any role that contains
Tula's magic.

Tula

I long to write like Heredia,
but what do I know of great cities
and the wide lives
of men?

I cannot write panoramas
of history — my narrow view
is framed by rigid window bars
and the songs of one tiny
caged bird.

I'm just a silenced girl.
My stories are simple tales
of emotion.

Will my words always be
glowing coals
instead of leaping
flames?

Tula

There is an opening
in the orphanage wall.
On a revolving wooden shelf,
gifts from the outside world
are received.

Each time the shelf spins,
I rush to see the surprises.
Townsfolk donate cakes, coins,
and clothing — small gifts that twirl
into this isolated orphanage
from beyond the high wall
of carved stone.

One day, the spinning shelf screams
and I'm the first to arrive. I discover
an infant, squirming
and squalling
on the polished circle
of time-smoothed wood.

The shrieking baby's arrival
is eerie. It seems unnatural,
until I peer through the gap
in the wall and see a girl
around my own age.

She is elegantly dressed,
but she weeps like a beggar
as she rushes away.
When she glances back
over her silk-clad shoulder,
her face is as pale
as a cloud.

She lifts a finger to her lips,
and I understand that she
is asking me to keep a secret.

She has abandoned her own
newborn infant.
Why? How?

Tula

I seize the baby and hold him close.
He falls silent, breathing against me.

When I gaze down at his black eyes
and warm cinnamon-hued skin,
I can hear a story unfolding . . .

The mother looked Spanish.
The father must be African.
This child was abandoned
simply because
he is brown.

The Nuns

Now that Tula knows

why most of the orphans

are given to us, she is desolate.

How can it be?

She wants to know

if the baby's parents are in love.

Is the father a freed man or a slave?

She asks the same questions

over and over,

and we give the same answer,

our true one —

we don't know.

All we know

is that most of the orphans we care for

are not really orphans, but children

with living parents who reject them

out of ignorant fear.

So many people

have not yet learned

that souls have no color

and can never

be owned.

Tula

Where can I put this mountain
of grief
and rage?

Sadness needs a papery home,
but my borrowed feather pen
is not skillful enough
to tell such a horrible
true tale.

It is a story far more monstrous
than any gruesome legend
of vampires
or werewolves.

Part Three
The Marriage Market

1828

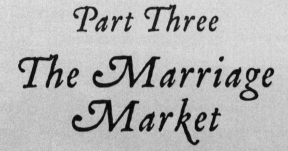

Tula

With the moon as my audience,
I whisper the tragedy
of abandoned babies
in every form I can imagine—
rhymed and free verse,
a story, an essay, a play . . .

But my words are never
strong enough
or public enough
to bring justice
for brown orphans.

If I ever find the courage
to reveal their secret openly,
will readers be brave enough
to listen
and care?

Tula

The only thing I can change
is myself. There is no way to alter
the orphans' loss, or my own
sorrowful home.

Fourteen is such a cruel birthday.
My mother and grandfather
are already planning
to auction me away
to the highest-bidding
rich man.

Mamá

The older Tula grows,
the more outcast she feels,
complaining that I permit her only
to spend time with her little brother.

She insists that she needs friends,
so I invite her cousin Rosa
and an acquaintance named Lola,
so that all three girls can laugh, sing,
play the piano, and practice
flirtatious dance steps.

When I hear the girls whispering
and giggling, I feel a burst of relief,
knowing there is still a chance
that my strange daughter
might turn out to be
normal.

Tula

The human mind is a garden.
Stories are tiny seeds that grow,
yet each evening, we inhale the ash
from my charred forest of pages.

Burning the poems—and pretending
that I've lost all interest in books—
is the only way to keep peace
in my mother's angry presence.

Now, when she calls me *profesora,*
I smile and claim that I am not smart
and plain, like a female professor.
If she calls me masculine, I wear
my best lace, flutter a flowery silk fan,
and keep myself silent, wishing
that I could openly state my truth:
I don't want to be a man,
just a woman
with a voice.

Manuel

Some of Tula's verses don't rhyme,
and there are oddly paired images:
butterflies in cemeteries,
and swans that float
on lakes of sadness . . .

Tula writes about equality
for slaves
and equality
for women.

When she writes about love,
her words are knives that pierce
my future. If women gain the freedom
to choose their own husbands,
will any pretty girl ever
choose me?

Caridad

Freely.

Part of life.

Secret words.

Give.

Future.

Lively.

Love.

Equality.

The slivers of talk I overhear

in this smoky kitchen

are just as sour-sweet

as the peel of an orange

left behind, after everyone else

has eaten.

I stay where I am for a long time,

nibbling the harsh fruit,

tasting the ashes

of poems.

Mamá

I have not forgotten how it feels

to be fourteen

and lonely,

so I must speak to my father soon,

very soon.

Tula needs a wealthy husband

now,

right now,

before she tries to choose her own,

the way I did, without any regard

for her family's

finances.

Tula

I feel at home, choosing to live
inside my own imagination,
savage
and natural,
yet I also long to be honest
about my desire
to love
and be loved.

Am I an unearthly creature,
part vampire, part werewolf?

Or perhaps, as Mamá accuses,
poetry is my beastly mind's
only curse.

Mamá

Honest, kind, and courageous.
Those are the charming qualities
Tula begs her grandfather to choose
when he selects her husband.

But he has already decided.
He's promised Tula's hand
to the most powerful man in town,
a rich merchant who won't refuse
such a beautiful young wife,
along with the generous dowry
my father offers in exchange
for the tidy arrangement.

My two love-marriages are proof
that romance alone cannot buy joy.
My first husband died too soon,
and the second spends all his time
far from home, as if to avoid Tula's
unhappiness, and my own.

Tula

The sun is a ghost.
My feelings are phantoms.

Suddenly, I am engaged
to a stranger.

No natural words
are enormous enough
to describe the gigantic sky
where I would escape
if I could fly.

I strive to imagine
that my profitable marriage
will turn out to be romantic—
an adventure, not a business deal,
not this hard, metallic,
commercial transfer
of female
merchandise.

The Nuns

Tula comes to us with her sorrow,
but this time we cannot help her.

If everyone obeyed God's golden rule,
then young girls would be the ones
to choose suitably greedy wives
for arrogant old men.
How swiftly the laws
about marriage
would change!

But this rough world prefers
laws soaked in dirt, not airy ones
drenched in clear light.

Tula

Today I released
my caged goldfinch.

Mamá scolded me bitterly,
but I do not care, because today
one small, winged creature
has finally learned
how to fly!

As I gaze up at glowing sun rays,
I wonder how long it will be
until I grow brave enough
      to follow
the little bird's
      soaring
pathway . . .

Tula

Do free birds and beasts
ever lie awake, troubled
by questions of justice?
At bedtime, I struggle
to stop thinking
of bondage and liberty,
cruelty and kindness,
wrong and right . . .
but fierce cries
and clattering hoofbeats
from the cobblestone street
beyond my barred window
rattle into my mind
like drumbeats of wildly
pounding questions.

I am engaged to a slave owner.
How does he treat his slaves,
and how will he treat a newly
purchased wife?

Caridad

Tula joins me, and we sit
in the smoky kitchen,
murmuring questions
without answers.

Will the rebels ever win?
Is it possible that someday
slaves will be free,
and kings
will vanish,
and everyone will vote,
even women?

Tula

Secret conversations
with Caridad
leave me feeling hopeful.

But after the rebels have once again
been defeated, I slip back down
to my usual
gloomy thoughts,
followed by music and noise
with Rosa and Lola — parties, dances,
and strolls around the plaza . . .
but what use are the admiring gazes
of gallant young men when I'm already
promised
to a stranger?

Tula

Boys lose interest in me
once they hear my modern
opinions. I need to spend time
with people who agree with me
about freedom for all — books
can no longer be my only portals.

Manuel, always curious, helps me
venture along narrow alleyways
to secret *tertulia*s — banned meetings
where rebel-poets recite their own
dangerous verses, along with
the smuggled poetry of Heredia,
brave, forbidden poems,
powerful ones, verses that burst
with possibilities.

Will I ever be bold enough
to read my own rhymes out loud,
in public?

Manuel

I risk my life for Tula's love
of verse.

Heredia is not just an abolitionist,
but an *independista,* promoting
the independence of Cuba.
My sister and I could be charged
with treason — arrest, torture,
exile, even execution . . .

We risk everything,
all for the crime of listening
to poems.

But Heredia has influenced me
as much as Tula. Lacking her talent
for flowery words, I hope to work
in some other way as a champion
of the twin causes — freedom

for slaves, and freedom
from kings.

Tula has a third cause,
all her own. No one agrees,
not even the rebels.
If women could choose
their own husbands,
and vote, and be elected,
wouldn't their sweet natures
grow just as rude and unruly
as men's?

Tula

My life is a balancing act
as dangerous as any carnival
performance. I roam back and forth
between banned poetry readings,
elegant parties, Caridad's kitchen,
the nuns' library, and my own
exhilarating orphan theater.

With my thoughts forced into secrecy,
I have entered a phase of legends.
The orphans perform plays inspired
by folktales—such a wonderful
way to hide
my true meanings!

There is one tale about
an ugly vulture with a kind heart,
and another about a tiny rabbit
who dreams of growing up to be
as strong and brave

as a lion,

and there is the wistful tale

of an earthbound turtle

who believes he can learn

how to fly.

Perhaps I'm as foolish

as that clumsy old turtle,

but I do believe that someday

silenced words

will rise

and glide.

The Orphans

Tula's legends about snakes
terrify us. A huge serpent chants
lullabies so sweet that birds in flight
fall asleep and tumble down
from the sky.

Yet somehow, at the same time,
that same legend also satisfies us,
because in the end, the snake
is transformed
into a skinny
palm tree
with no
voice
at all.

In Tula's legends, gentle creatures
are always rewarded by speaking,
while cruel ones are punished
with silence.

Tula

I think of my feather pen
as something magical
that still belongs
to a wing.

All I need
is paper, ink,
and the courage
to let wild words soar.

Caridad

Tula performs her secret plays
in the garden, just for me.

The words are so quiet
that I have to listen
with all my heart—
not just my ears.

The tale of the turtle
is my favorite.

If such a slow, awkward creature
can hope to grow swift wings,
then I can at least try to move
my own two weary
human legs.

Tula

Caridad is gone! She quit her job
and fled without a farewell, leaving
nothing but a wordless
mist of hope.

Mamá falls into a rage, blaming me,
just as she blames me for so much—
her nerves, her headaches, her fear
that I will gain such a bold reputation
that the fiancé I've never seen
will reject me before
our first meeting.

None of that matters.
All I can think of is dear Caridad
in bright air,
soaring!

Mamá

My selfish daughter's punishment
for talking nonsense to the old cook
will be cooking.

As soon as Tula marries, her husband
will have to buy me a new cook,
two maids, a gardener, a fine
team of horses, a coachman,
and a stable boy . . .

In the meantime, let Tula
stew beans and scrub pots.
Maybe the grit and filth of a kitchen
will remind her that food, firewood,
and a respectable place
in society
are not free.

Caridad

I do not know where I'll go,
but I do know that words
helped me flee. My name
has always meant "charity,"
such a common name for slaves,
who receive
no charity at all.

But I did — first I received
freedom papers, and now,
so late in life, I've received
this winged-turtle liberty
of the mind,
a freedom so huge that it can never
be crowded onto anything as small
and fragile
as a page.

Tula

I seize the kitchen
as my own.

Chop, stir, scribble —
my punishment
is a blessing of privacy.
Mamá hardly ever steps into
the smoke, so I feel free
to keep my new pages,
instead of feeding them
to hungry flames.

When I ask my brother for help,
he agrees to hide my words in his room.
If Mamá finds the bundles of paper,
Manuel can pretend that my legends
are his. No one ever objects
to strange tales written
by a boy.

Tula

Caridad's act of independence
inspires me, just as my turtle tale
influenced her.

When I finally meet the gentleman
I'm expected to marry, he speaks
of nothing but mansions and jewels,
promising that we will travel to Paris,
attend dances, wear furs . . .

I smile politely, but a secret verse
grows in my mind, telling me to run,
join the nuns, flee to the library,
open my own book-shaped portal
to an imaginary world
of freedom
and fairness.

Tula

My wedding day is still many
long months away, so I shove all fear
out of my mind, determined to enjoy
my new cooking duties, as well as
the library, orphanage, poetry,
and friendly visits
with Rosa and Lola.

Every day, I imagine the true love
that my two girlfriends discuss
with such joy, yet I have no idea
what the word *amor* really means.
When Rosa introduces me to a boy
called Loynaz, I imagine that we
are in love.

Sweaty hands. Tumbling heartbeats.
Trembling voices.

If this is *amor,* then why

does it feel

just as troubling

as a simple case

of youthful

shyness?

Friendship — that is all I want

from Loynaz. All these other

turbulent feelings are too

mysterious. I'm too young

for love, too confused

for marriage.

Tula

Lola has eloped!
Rosa blames me for daring
to speak in praise of a future
when women will be able
to choose marriages
based on love.

I don't care
if I'm blamed.
One more caged bird
has escaped.

Lola is pale and her husband
is dark, but love has no limits—
of that much
I feel certain.

Tula

Rosa is so envious that she chooses
to betray my trust.

Like a spy, she takes her vicious gossip
to Mamá, reporting my harmless
flirtations with Loynaz.

I am accused
of improper behavior.

Rosa has transformed
our friendship
into cruelty.

Now she is suddenly
engaged to Loynaz,
while I must face Mamá's
fury.

Tula

My punishment
is drastic.

The marriage
will be rushed.

Only ninety days
of freedom
remain.
Ninety days.
Nothing.
No one
can help me.
I am
lost.

Tula

I can't do it.
I won't pretend
to love
a stranger.

I will not marry
a bank account
instead of
a human.

Mamá

My daughter is a clever girl,
but she is selfish and thinks only
of her own fantasies.

She has made such a show of flirting
with a boy who has nothing at all
to offer — no money, no property,
no fame.

As soon as Tula is profitably married,
her wild tantrums, these ridiculous pleas
for freedom,
will end.

All our lives will be peaceful
and prosperous.

Tula

I am alone
and my heart
is my own.

Loneliness.
Solitude.
The first is a curse,
the second a blessing.
I would rather be a hermit
than live with a stranger
who would make me feel
even more lonely
than when I am
truly
alone.

Tula

Monster!

Bookworm!

Unnatural!

Professor!

Genius!

Atheist!

The insults my mother screeches
have no limit.

Atheist? No. Love is God's
boldest creation.

Surely, angels on clouds
must gaze down and smile
each time a girl on earth
refuses a marriage
based on love's
absence.

Part Four
See Me as I Am
1829

Tula

The punishment for shunning
a forced marriage is being shunned.
Mamá sends me to live as a prisoner,
trapped in my grandfather's
fine marble mansion
on his lush green plantation,
surrounded by sugar
and slaves.

I am fifteen now, old enough
to know my own mind,
but my stern old *abuelito*
still treats me like a child,
or a monster.

He scolds and screams
until I long to die,
and then, suddenly,
after three months
of hateful insults

and endless arguments,
his raging heart fails,
and I am left feeling
truly monstrous.

I loved him, in the angry way
of young girls who love their families,
no matter how oppressive, no matter
how maddening.

Now I really do feel like *la loca,*
the crazy girl, a madwoman,
just as Mamá and *abuelito* accused.

At the funeral, I remain quiet
in my mother's infuriated presence.
She blames me for her father's death,
and even though I do feel shamefully
responsible for arguing, I also feel
absolutely certain
that my grandfather's angry heart
was his own.

Tula

At the reading of the will,
my mother learns that she has lost
her entire inheritance, and this time,
the loss really is my fault.

Houses, farms, gold — everything
will go to an uncle, simply because
I refused to be sold.
From beyond the grave,
my grandfather continues
to punish my mother
for defying him
so many years ago.

I try to feel sympathy for her,
but secretly, I'm so relieved
that I will never inherit sugar
and slaves.

Tula

Banished.

Outcast.

Rejected.

Forever.

Mamá won't allow me to come home.

She tells me to stay in the countryside

and rest. She thinks I'm hysterical.

She believes that I'm mad.

Why can't she see that I am

the sane one, and it's only

the bizarre rules of society

that are crazy?

My uncle, the new master

of this farm, is indifferent

to my presence, so I dwell

like a fairy-tale princess

in a palace, surrounded

by luxuries and caged

human lives.

Tula

The horror keeps me awake.

Even the house slaves fear me.

Cooks and maids never speak to me.

No one notices that I am not the one

who wields whips

and chains.

I cannot rest. I cannot write.

If my own unhappiness

could magically bring

my grandfather

back to life,

I would swiftly agree

to a future of married

misery.

Tula

When my gloating uncle leaves
to claim his other new properties,
I dare to explore the mansion.
Most of the rooms contain treasure:
books, paper, ink, pens . . .

Solitude.
Serenity.
It's no use —
I can't write;
I need to roam.

For the first time in my life,
I've been released from the walls
that trap women.

Alone, I venture outdoors, wandering
along muddy pathways, beside a river
so peaceful that I dream, and then
I swim . . .

Forests, coffee groves, guava thickets,
mango orchards. So much beauty,
so much life! Honeybee hives,
hummingbird nests, pink flamingos
and green parrots, a giant woodpecker
with a smooth ivory bill — each sight
is a marvel that deserves its own poem,
but all I can do is look and listen,
feeling serenaded by sound
and drenched in color
as I gather my skirts
to run freely
beneath wild flocks
of huge red macaws.

Has sunlight always
been this bright,
or were my mind
and my eyes
asleep?

Tula

My uncle stays far away,
leaving the mansion's inhabitants
uncertain. Cooks and maids grow
more confident, offering their names
and their stories.

They seem to know that I'm not
the proper lady I was trained
to be, but a half-wild creature,
a throwback to some other,
more natural time and place.

I perform plays, recite poems,
and then let my audience go about
their daily routines, without
any rules
made by me.

I want to tell all the slaves
that they are free to leave,

but I have
no authority.

A few flee at night,
while overseers are sleeping,
but most stay, convinced
that sooner or later
my uncle will return
and send slave hunters
to chop off the feet of captives
who've shown that they know
how to run.

Sometimes, fear
is the most powerful
weapon.

Tula

I leave the sad mansion

to roam tangled jungles,

tranquil orchards, dark caves,

and my own silent fear

of never knowing

how to live

in a world

where I don't belong.

Nature is a sanctuary. Wilderness

invites me. All I need is this leafy

green

pathway

toward truth . . .

but each time I go back to the house

that I can never think of as home,

I feel jolted by the sight of girls

my own age, scarred by whips

instead of words.

Tula

So many of the babies
on this plantation
are brown.

In the city, they would be orphans,
but here, they stay with their mothers.

When my grandfather was young
and strong, did he rule
like a brutal king?

Are any of the slaves
in the sugar fields
my relatives?

Tula

Disturbed and desolate,
I roam country roads
crowded with wanderers —
muleteers and musicians,
vendors, herders, hunters,
and traveling magicians,
all singing their rhythmic
wayfaring songs.

I dream of fleeing to Havana,
the biggest city on the island,
where I could work as a tutor,
earn my own money, travel,
see Niagara Falls,
meet Heredia . . .

Tula

One morning, on a green hill

beside a forest, an old woman

leans from the open doorway

of her raggedly thatched hut.

She calls out, inviting me

to share her dinner

and a story.

The meal is just yams and corn,

but her tale is a familiar legend

that seems to spring from the roots

of my own life: Once there was a king

who kept his son hidden in a tree

so that the prince could never

meet a girl and risk

the heartbreak of love.

Birds taught the tree-boy

their language of songs.

A hawk showed the prince

how to hunt, owls offered lessons
in wisdom, parrots taught the art
of cheerfulness, and doves spoke
of love. One day, all the birds
joined together
and lifted the tree-boy,
flying with him balanced
between their wings.

They flew and flew, until finally
they reached a far kingdom,
where they dropped the prince
onto a treetop. There, a beautiful
young princess lived in isolation
because her father, too, imagined
that young people can be protected
from the pain of finding
and losing
love.

Tula

The old woman's tale
of lonely tree-children
stays with me until gradually,
day after day, the storyteller's
friendly hut becomes my refuge.

It is also my inspiration.
I gather the old woman's stories
like sour green fruits that can be eaten
later, once their sweetness has grown
full and ripe.

Other wanderers come to the hut
for tales and companionship.
I meet farmers with sun-withered skin,
children with bright, eager eyes,
and Sab — the storyteller's godson,
a half-African freed slave,
flame-scarred
and troubled.

Sab

My name is Bernabé, but ever since
I ran into a fiery hut to rescue
a burning child, everyone calls me Sab,
from *saber* — "to know." People seem
to imagine that my scars
give me wisdom.

I am not a storyteller,
but I will tell you about my life,
so that you and the other wanderers
who visit my godmother
will understand
and believe
the powerful nature
of love.

I was raised along with my owner's
daughter, Carlota, who taught me
how to read, and how to dream

of a normal future together,
dark and light joined forever,
without any hatred, sadness,
or fear.

We were inseparable.
We were happy. We promised
that someday we would marry
and have children of our own . . .
but that hopeful age ended
along with childhood's
shared laughter.

Now we are grown,
and I still love Carlota
with all my heart, but she plans
to marry a gentleman who gallops
around the countryside
on a spirited horse
that makes him
look brave.

After the fire, when Carlota's father
freed me, he gave me this gentle pony
and one imperial lottery ticket — *see,
it's a winning ticket, worth a fortune!*

Her father gave me instructions, too.
He ordered me to ride all the way
to Havana to claim my prize,
enough gold to buy a house
and a business, in that rich city
where freed slaves flourish
like vines.

He told me to ride far away
and never return to this valley.
He imagined that wealth could cure
my lovesickness, but he's wrong.
They're all wrong, the greedy fools
who believe that an absence of love
can be purchased.

Tula

Sab's tale of rejection
by his childhood sweetheart
is so emotional that I feel
both anger and envy.

I long for love, yet Carlota
has sent her true love away.
Did she stop caring about Sab
merely because his skin is brown
or because his face is scarred?

But what do I know of loyalty?
All I've seen of love is the daydream
described in romantic novels.

What about reality? It's never
as simple as a fantasy. Is there
any way for Sab's tale of loss
to end
hopefully?

Tula

During my next visit
to the storyteller's hut,
I meet Carlota and her gallant
gentleman — she is lovely,
and he is so handsome
that I find myself imagining
I am the fortunate girl on his arm,
ready to travel with him to Paris
and Madrid, where we could visit
salons and I would have a chance
to meet Europe's great poets . . .

Swept away by fantasy,
I convince myself that any man
who is charming must also be honest
and courageous, a hero of justice
like Heredia.

Sab

I have planted a moonlight garden
for Carlota.

All the flowers bloom only
at night.

While she is lost
in sleep,
the fragrance of jasmine
and angel's trumpet
will blossom
and flow
up to her window
into her dreams,
helping her dream
of love.

Tula

I've been transformed
into a messenger. Sab has asked me
to carry heartfelt love notes.

In the first passionate letter,
he begs Carlota to wake up
and gaze at her moonlit garden
of night-blooming magic . . .
but her blunt reply is a series
of commands: Go. Flee. Never
try to visit me again. Send no more
flowery notes. Forget our friendship.
We were just children.
It was not love.

Sab

Instead of another doomed note,

this time I send a bracelet

woven

of my own hair,

to remind Carlota

how it felt

when our two small heads

touched

and all the rest

of this vast

spinning world

seemed so distant

and powerless.

Tula

My role as a messenger feels
oddly familiar. I am like Manuel,
a smuggler of words, as I sneak
back and forth, followed
by *Leal*—"Loyal"—a little dog
who chooses to regard me
as his friend, even though
he belongs to the storyteller.

Instead of answering Sab's woven plea,
Carlota confides in me, sharing anxieties.
Her father recently placed all his wealth
into a risky investment, and now he is
suddenly bankrupt and she is poor,
and the gentleman Carlota loves
turns out to be greedy.
As soon as he heard the news
of her family's misfortune,
he told her that he no longer

has any interest
in marrying her.

Foolish Carlota is unwilling
to forget him,
just as Sab is unable
to forget her.

Why did I ever imagine
that love
could be simple?

Sab

I envy my little horse.
He never despairs.
He does not care
if I feel sadness
or joy.

He carries me
without questions,
treating me
like his friend,
instead of a burden.

I envy the trees
that grow
at crossroads.
They are never
forced
to decide
which way
to go . . .

Tula

How could I ever
have pictured myself
in love with Carlota's
greedy gentleman?

There is nothing gentle
about a selfish passion
for money.

Sab is the only man
I have ever known
who shares my dreams
and my nature.

Sab is the only one
I can truly love
forever.

Sab

There is a vast cave
near the storyteller's hut—a huge,
mysterious chain of caverns
where her Ciboney Indian
ancestors
lived long ago.

Weighed down by my visions
of an unhappy future, I wander
through the maze of caves,
with only a small candle
to light my way.

One chamber resembles a palace
carved from sapphires
and diamonds.

In another chamber,
ancient people left bright
red and black paintings

of frogs and birds
on water-smoothed walls.

In some chambers, jagged crystals
are shaped like heads and hands,
as if spirits
had turned to stone.

Beyond the eleventh chamber,
no one has ever ventured.
It is said to be the jaw
of hell.

I peer into the gloom, then turn
and make my way back outdoors,
to a sunlit moment
of decision.

I will ask Tula to marry the man
who is loved by Carlota, leaving
my sweetheart free to remember
that she once loved me.

Tula

No brilliant playwright
could ever have imagined
a more ironic
and devastating scene.

Just after I realize that I've fallen
in love with Sab, he asks me
to marry
someone else.

My answer will have to shatter
his scarred heart
along with my broken one.

If it's true — as the old storyteller
promises — that souls can rise and soar
in dreams, then I must be a night-flying
bird with clipped wings. Will I ever
be brave enough to sing
in sunlight?

Sab

Tula has refused to marry
the man on the spirited horse.

She calls my request horrible,
insisting that marriage
without love
is just one more
twisted
form
of slavery.

She is right.
I am human.

Tula

We carry our tangled emotions
to the storyteller, whose age gives
the wisdom of experience,
but in place of clear advice,
Sab's godmother gives us
a parable, a story
about a house filled
with mirrors.

By the time her tale ends,
Sab and I both understand
that we are living reflections
of each other's
freedom dreams.

Sab

When I asked Tula to marry

the gallant gentleman,

I imagined that she loved

no one,

but my godmother's tale

of mirrors

helps me see that Tula

loves me

and I have been

cruel,

just as Carlota is cruel

to me.

Tula

Love is as tricky as a wall
of mirrors that make
narrow hallways
seem open
and wide.

Sab is startled when I invite him
to marry me, but I must admit
that I am not completely
surprised
by how readily
he refuses me.

His devotion to a childhood love
is as much a part of his goodness
as the courage that sent him
running through flames
to save
a burning child.

Sab

If I could love Tula,
I would.

But love
is a wildly
unpredictable
hurricane wind,
not a swirling
blue ocean
with peaceful
shores.

Tula

There was a time
just a few hours ago
when I felt breathless
with hope
for a future with Sab,
but now I feel smothered
by grief.

I miss the company
of orphans.

No one else has ever seen me
as I really am — an outcast,
a wanderer, condemned
to explore
the unknown world
of human emotions . . .

Sab

We remain friends,
close companions.

Tula and I agree
that we will never grow bitter,
never see each other as enemies.

If I could have a sister,
I would choose Tula.

If I could plant a garden
with wings, the feathers
would be her wandering
words.

Tula

I long for love's joy
for myself, but I also wish for Sab's
true happiness, even though
it means that he will find joy
with someone else.

So, while he dreams
of a thousand ways
to change Carlota's
rigid mind,
I dream
of a million ways
to change my own
stubborn heart.

Sab

If Carlota's father's fortune
was restored, she could marry
her gentleman and she would be
happy.

With no other way to help her
feel joy, I resolve to give her
the only object of value
that I have ever held
in my hand.

This winning lottery ticket
means nothing to me,
but it will mean everything
to Carlota, who longs to regain
her value as a marketable
bride.

Tula

Sab's plan is both generous
and hideous.

His only joy will grow from knowing
that his childhood love is happy
with someone else.

My own future is tragic, too.
All I can do is give ugly sorrow
a comforting home on paper,
folded
and tucked away —
my hidden treasury
of secrets.

Part Five

The Hotel
of Peace

1836

Tula

Perhaps it is true that time
heals love's wounds,
but for me, poetry
has always been
the swiftest medicine.

Seven long years ago,
unable to stay in the valley
where Sab loved another,
I begged a ride on a caravan
of musicians and rode, swaying
in their brightly painted wagon,
all the way to Havana, as I listened
to the sad-happy lyrics of songs
about love found and lost—
rhymed songs
wrapped
in joyful music.

Tula

Life in this huge, anonymous city
has taught me how to survive
on my own, thinking independently
and earning my own salary
as a tutor.

Plans for a few healing verses
about my turbulent feelings for Sab
have grown into a novel, a whole book—
although I've not yet been brave enough
to set the words down on paper.

I carry them around in my
heart and mind
   like wild birds
that fly in all directions
      without any fear
  of being unable to return
to the safety
of a nest.

Tula

City life is a whirl of poetry readings
and forbidden *tertulias*, gatherings
where young and old, rich and poor,
male and female, dark and light —
runaway slaves and freed ones,
former masters and former
servants — all take turns
sharing secret verses
rooted in startling
new ideas.

Each evening, I go home
with a mind that glows
in the light of words,
which leap
like flames . . .

Tula

After reading a few
of my boldest new verses
in public, I begin to wonder
about the timid past
and the courageous future.

All the orphans I knew are grown
by now, perhaps writing and acting
their own daring parts . . .

But what about Sab—
is he happy?

And how can Carlota
ever be content in a marriage
to a man who loves only
her money?

Manuel

During visits to Havana,
I'm shocked by my sister's
independence, but also inspired.
If a woman can shed all the whims
of tradition, then so can a man.
So can I.

When Mamá tries to choose
my wife, I'll defy her . . .

In the meantime, I need to warn Tula
that our mother is already arranging
another profitable engagement
for her.

Tula

My brother's warning
does not frighten me.
I am twenty-two years old,
and no one can tell me
how to marry.

Last night, at a poetry reading,
soldiers sent the audience scurrying
for safety. I had just glimpsed Caridad
in the crowd, moving toward me,
but she escaped, and I escaped too.

Now I'm convinced that I must
go overseas, to live and write
in exile, like Heredia.

There is no other way to tell
a truthfully balanced tale
of slavery.

Caridad

In Havana, I've earned a living
making sweet cakes.

A portion of my baking
goes to a convent, for the orphans,
and a portion of each evening
is given over to poetry, as I listen
while orphans read to me.

I almost had a chance to visit
with Tula and let her know
how much her winged turtle
meant to me.

Even though we could not
speak, I saw her smile.
I think she knows.

Tula

Can a woman ever write
the true thoughts of a man?
Will I be able to show Sab's
soul on paper?
Can a free person
really understand one whose dreams
must fly up and soar
high above the depths
of slavery?

Is my imagination enough,
or do I need to add the ways
in which I myself
have felt enslaved?

I must be honest, writing myself
into the story, revealing
all my secrets.

Tula

Manuel and I have bought
passage on a ship to Spain,
with a stop in France.
He warns me that Mamá
and our stepfather will be
on the same ship, but I know
that I can avoid their tricks.
I am strong.

People in small boats call out,
then turn and rhythmically row
back to shore. Sailors sing,
while I watch the sea.

With my face to the wind,
I dream of Sab, both the real man
and my novel.

This will not be a book
about the whips and chains

of slavery. It will simply be
a gentle
tale of love.

If the story is seen
as proof that human souls
are transparent and free
of all color, class, and gender,
then I will know
that I have succeeded
in showing how people
are all equal
and should always
be equally
free.

Tula

The novel will have to wait —
this blue sea fills my mind
with poetry.

When a hurricane overtakes
the ship, Manuel and Mamá
flee to their cabins, but I perch
on deck
in a double tempest.

I live at the center of two storms,
one of wind, the other a hurricane
of the spirit, a storm of emotions
that helps me fight back
with strong words
whenever life is unfair
and I feel
powerless.

Tula

Passage across the sea
is long and exhausting,
but I feel so exhilarated!
We've arrived at the French
river port of Bordeaux,
and I've managed to ignore
my mother's efforts to talk
about another engagement.

Eager to write about Sab,
I sit at a little desk in a small room
in a hotel called *Paz*—"Peace."

I have a feather pen,
and a window
with a view of sky.

What more do I need?
I don't know how my book
will end.

All I know is that love
is not the modern invention
of rebellious young girls.

Love is ancient.
A legend.
The truth.

Historical Note

The Lightning Dreamer is historical fiction. I have tried to present realistic portraits of Gertrudis Gómez de Avellaneda and her family, but I have also taken great liberties, imagining many details.

Gertrudis Gómez de Avellaneda (1814–1873):

Born in Puerto Príncipe (now Camagüey), Cuba, Avellaneda was variously known by her childhood nickname Tula, the pen name *La Peregrina* ("The Wanderer"), and *La Avellaneda*. Because her mother regarded reading and writing as unladylike, young Tula wrote stories about giants and vampires in secret, then burned them.

Sab, Carlota, the old storyteller, and the greedy gentleman are actually fictional characters from Avellaneda's groundbreaking abolitionist novel, *Sab*. Biographers believe these characters were inspired by real people Avellaneda met at the age of fifteen, when she was sent to a country estate "to rest" after refusing an arranged marriage. I have imagined Avellaneda's encounters with her own fictional characters, borrowing many aspects from *Sab* and inventing others.

During her lifetime, Avellaneda was celebrated as one of the world's most prominent female writers. Known primarily as a poet and playwright, she chose lyrical prose for her boldest work. Written in the romantic, melodramatic style of the time, *Sab* was one of the world's first abolitionist novels and the earliest one written in Spanish. *Sab* is also the only known Latin American abolitionist novel that combines proemancipation views with feminist themes. Banned in Cuba, *Sab* was published in Spain in 1841, eleven years before the American publication of *Uncle Tom's Cabin* by Harriet Beecher Stowe.

Avellaneda began writing *Sab* when she was only twenty-two, at the Hotel de la Paz (Hotel of Peace) in Bordeaux, France. The interracial love story in *Sab* was considered so scandalous that numerous copies were purchased and destroyed by Avellaneda's relatives in Spain. Despite their efforts to suppress the book, Avellaneda's brother, Manuel, remained loyal and brave, smuggling her banned books between Spain and Cuba.

Sab became influential throughout Europe and the Americas, inspiring compassion for slaves and for young girls forced to marry strangers. Avellaneda not only believed that slaves should be freed and women should choose their own husbands; she was bold enough to portray interracial marriage and voluntary marriage as completely normal. She felt that regardless of ancestry, all Cubans belonged to a rich cultural blend of Spanish, African, and indigenous Ciboney-Taíno Indian origins. Her conviction that all should be equally proud of every ethnic component of a shared society was an idea so original and courageous that it helped readers question the way they viewed slavery, interracial marriage, and the broader issue of voluntary marriage. By telling a simple love story, Avellaneda conveyed her dream of universal dignity, freedom, and equal rights for men and women of all races.

Avellaneda spent most of her adult life in Spain, where her writing often focused on marriages arranged for profit, a tradition she viewed as the marketing of teenage girls. With essays such as *"Capacidad de las mujeres para el gobierno"* ("Capacity of Women for Government"), she confirmed her role as one of the world's earliest and most outspoken feminist authors.

While Avellaneda achieved remarkable literary success, her personal life was plagued by tragedy. After refusing two potentially profitable arranged marriages, she was shunned and ridiculed by disappointed relatives. Later, she fell in love with a man who refused to marry her because she was poor and another who abandoned her after she gave birth out of wedlock. She eventually married twice, but her first husband died of illness and the second was stabbed during a duel with a heckler who had tossed a cat onto the stage during a performance of one of her controversial plays.

The greatest disappointment of Avellaneda's professional life was her exclusion from the all-male Royal Spanish Academy. Without membership, she could not receive the financial benefits granted to male writers. She satirized her rejection as the "Bearded Academy's" policy of discrimination against anyone who could not shave.

In 1859, Avellaneda returned to Cuba, where she established a literary magazine for women. In 1864, on her way back to Spain, she visited Niagara Falls in memory of José María Heredia, whose poetry and abolitionist views had inspired her.

During her lifetime, Avellaneda's ideas were considered shocking, but her clear vision of racial and gender equality was eventually accepted. Cuban slaves were emancipated; public employment and public schools were integrated, although private parochial schools remained segregated throughout the first half of the twentieth century. Interracial marriage became common throughout the Spanish-speaking Caribbean, now home to one of the world's most culturally mixed populations. The archaic custom of forcing young girls into financially motivated arrangements was gradually replaced by voluntary marriages based on love.

José María Heredia (1803-1839):

Heredia[*] is regarded as Avellaneda's mentor, even though they never met. As Cuba's first Romantic era poet, Heredia paired his abolitionist views with the goal of independence from colonial Spain. He was still a teenager when he became a founder of *Los Caballeros Racionales* (The Rational Gentlemen), a nonviolent branch of the secret society called *Los Soles y Rayos de Bolívar* (The Suns and Rays of Bolívar). Heredia was forced into exile after he was betrayed by a spy. He escaped from Cuba disguised as a sailor, lived in Boston, wrote poetry at Niagara Falls, taught Spanish in New York, and became a diplomat and judge in Mexico. Known as *El Homero Cubano* (The Cuban Homer) or *El Cantor del Niágara* (The Singer of Niagara), Heredia inspired later generations of Cuban abolitionists and independence advocates.

[*] Often confused with his cousin, the Cuban French poet José María de Heredia (1842–1905)

The following excerpt from the poem *"A Emilia"* ("To Emilia") is representative of Heredia's work:

. . . bajo el hermoso desnublado cielo
no pude resolverme a ser esclavo,
ni consentir que todo en la natura
fuese noble y feliz, menos el hombre.

. . . under the beautiful clear sky
I could not accept slavery,
nor regard all of nature
as noble and happy, except man.

The Writing of Gertrudis Gómez de Avellaneda

PROSE

Excerpts from the abolitionist novel *Sab*:

¿Quién se acordará de tu color al verte amar tanto y sufrir tanto?

Who will remember your color when they see how greatly you love and suffer?

Los hombres dirán que yo he sido infeliz por mi culpa; porque he soñado los bienes que no estaban en mi esfera, porque he querido mirar al sol, como el águila . . . ¿Es culpa mía si Dios me ha dotado de un corazón y de un alma?

Men will say it is my own fault that I have been unhappy; because I have dreamed of things beyond my reach, because I have longed to gaze on the sun, like an eagle . . . Is it my fault if God has given me a heart and a soul?

¡Oh! ¡Las mujeres! ¡Pobres y ciegas víctimas! Como los esclavos, ellas arrastran pacientemente su cadena y bajan la cabeza bajo el yugo de las leyes humanas.

Oh! Women! Poor blind victims! Like slaves, they stoically

drag their chains and lower their heads beneath the yoke of human laws.

POETRY

Excerpt from *"Las contradicciones"* ("Contradictions"):

. . . Ni libre soy, ni la prisión me encierra;
Veo sin luz, sin voz hablar ansío . . .

Busco el peligro cuando auxilio imploro;
Al sentirme morir me encuentro fuerte . . .

. . . I am neither free, nor locked in prison;
I see without light, without a voice I long to speak . . .

I seek danger while pleading for rescue;
Feeling doomed I discover my strength . . .

Excerpt from *"A mi jilguero"* ("To My Goldfinch"):

Libertad y amor te falta;
¡libertad y amor te doy!
¡Salta, pajarillo, salta,
que no tu tirana soy!

Salida franca,
ya tienes, mira,

goza, respira . . .

libre eres ya.

You lack liberty and love;
I give you liberty and love!
Leap, little bird, leap,
I am not your tyrant!

A clear exit
is yours, look,
enjoy, breathe . . .
you are already free.

Excerpt from *"La noche de insomnio y el alba"* ("The Night of Insomnia and the Dawn"):

Noche

Triste

Viste

Ya,

Aire,

Cielo,

Suelo,

Mar.

Brindándole

Al mundo
Profundo
Solaz,
Derraman
Los sueños
Beleños
De paz.

Night
Sad
Already
You've seen
Air,
Sky,
Soil,
Sea.
Offering
To the world
Profound
Solace,
Spilling
Dreams
The potion
Of peace.

Excerpt from *"Romance"* ("Ballad"):

Canto porque hay en los seres
Sus condiciones precisas:
Corre el agua, vuela el ave,
Silba el viento, y el Sol brilla.

Canto sin saber yo propia
Lo que el canto significa,
Y si al mundo, que lo escucha,
Asombro o lástima inspira.

I sing because each being
Has its purpose:
Water flows, birds fly,
Wind whistles, and Sun shines.

I sing without knowing
What my song means,
And whether the listening world
Is amazed or wounded.

References

Avellaneda, Gertrudis Gómez de. *Cartas ineditas*. Madrid: Fundación Madrid, 1975.

————. *Poemas*. Barcelona: Linkgua Ediciones, 2007.

————. *Sab*. Madrid: Catedra Ediciones, 1998.

————. *Sab and Autobiography*. Trans. and ed. by Nina M. Scott. Austin: University of Texas Press, 1993.

Bravo-Villasante, Carmen. *Una vida rómantica — La Avellaneda*. Barcelona: EDHASA, 1967.

Harter, Hugh A. *Gertrudis Gómez de Avellaneda*. Boston: Twayne, 1981.

Heredia, José María. *Antología Herediana*. Havana: Imprenta El Siglo, 1939.

————. *Obra poética*. Havana: Letras Cubanas, 1993.

————. *Selected Poems*. Trans. Angel Aparicio Laurencio. Miami: Ediciones Universal, 1970.

Lazo, Raimundo. *Gertrudis Gómez de Avellaneda, la mujer y la poetisa lírica*. Mexico City: Editorial Porrúa, 1990.

Pastor, Brígida M. *Fashioning Feminism in Cuba and Beyond: The Prose of Gertrudis Gómez de Avellaneda*. New York: Peter Lang, 2003.

Acknowledgments

I thank God for the magic of words that travel across centuries and oceans.

Lifelong love and thanks to Curtis—without you, I would be unable to write.

I am grateful to my editor, Reka Simonsen, and the entire publishing team at Harcourt, especially Jeannette Larson, Lisa DiSarro, Jennifer Groves, Elizabeth Tardiff, Amy Carlisle, and Adah Nuchi.